The Philips Family Legacy

by

Brian Anderson

Authored by:

Brian Keith Anderson Keeper of stories. Weavers of memory. Descendant of Willie Jane Phillips—and steward of her legacy. With heartfelt dedication to the Phillips, Brown, Anderson, Adams, and Poff lines.

This book is dedicated to:

Willie Jane Phillips (1908-1991) – my paternal grandmother, Born and buried in Hillsboro, Tennessee, she carried the family line with quiet strength, warm hands, and a soul stitched in perseverance. Her story is not just written here—it shaped every page that follows. Through joys and trials, through five children and decades of grace, she became the thread that held our family quilt together. This book honors her memory, preserves her legacy, and offers it to all who walk the Phillips path after her.

Table of Contents

Preface

Some stories are found in dusty boxes and brittle photographs. Others are stitched into the silence between porchlight conversations and graveside prayer. This book began not with certainty—but with longing.

As I walked the grounds of Wesley Chapel, stood at my parents' resting place, and felt the weight of generations press gently on my shoulders, I knew something had to be preserved. Not just names and dates—but character, sacrifice, and spirit.

The Phillips line—my own blood—runs deep across Tennessee soil. From land grants and war service to church halls and garden fences, they lived lives both ordinary and

remarkable. My grandmother, Willie Jane Phillips, is the heart of this manuscript. Her quiet strength, steady hands, and decades of presence gave shape to our family quilt. Through her, I see the thread that reaches back to Johnson and William Phillips, and forward into the unknown years of my descendants.

This book is not comprehensive—but it is careful. It is not perfect—but it is personal. What follows is a blend of history and heart, built with help from kind souls, community wisdom, and my own aching need to remember.

I offer it humbly to anyone who carries Phillips in their name—or in their spirit.

Introduction

Every family has a beginning—roots buried deep in soil and memory. For the Phillips line, which begins unfolds in the gentle hills of Tennessee, where the names etched in stone tell more than just dates. They speak of perseverance, migration, service, and home.

This book traces a line that reaches from Willie Jane Phillips, my paternal grandmother, and the emotional heart of this story, back to the earliest known ancestors—Johnson and William Phillips, pioneers who carved a legacy from post-Revolution frontierland. Through carefully gathered records, photographs, and personal recollections, these chapters seek to illuminate not just who these individuals were, but why they mattered.

In the pages ahead, I have arranged our journey through time, beginning with myself, then my father Robert Kenneth Anderson Sr., followed by Willie Jane, and each head of house moving backward across generations. Later chapters revisit each figure with deeper narrative, allowing their character to emerge through context, choices, and the quiet details that genealogy often overlooks.

This manuscript is equal parts tribute and testament. It carries my voice—but it is built with many hands: from my niece's editorial guidance to Bob Sherwood's local insight, and from photographs unnamed to stories rediscovered. Together, we have stitched a quilt of memory that holds together place, name, and meaning.

If you are a Phillips by blood or by spirit, this book is your inheritance too.

Chapter 1: Seeds of the Past – Tracing the Earliest Phillips

"As I stood at the Cemetery, camera in hand, the wind whispered through the cedar. That moment became more than a photograph—it became the starting line of memory, the ground from which this entire work would grow."

This photograph was taken near Wesley Chapel, Tennessee. I stood in quiet thought among stones marked with names I knew, and some I had yet to learn—
That day, I didn't just feel connected—
I felt called.   January 2021

Author: Brian Keith Anderson

Chapter 1: *The Legacy Keeper – Brian Keith Anderson*

I did not set out to author a book. I set out to remember. The path to this manuscript was carved one photo at a time—faded faces with no names, hand-scratched birth records, cemetery visits where silence said more than marble could. As the pages filled, I realized I was not just telling a family story, I was stitching my own role into it.

My name is **Brian Keith Anderson**, son of Robert Kenneth Anderson Sr., grandson of Willie Jane Phillips. I was born into the Tennessee earth where most of these stories unfolded, raised on porchlight wisdom and the subtle strength of people who did not ask for history to notice them—but earned its respect anyway.

The Phillips line runs through me like tobacco roots—quiet, firm, resilient. Their resilience and the grace of my grandmother gave me the lens through which I now see every photograph, every faint document, every unanswered question. This manuscript is my way of saying *thank you* to those who came before and remember me to those who are yet unborn.

Willie Jane, my grandmother, in Hillsboro First United Methodist Church, the same soil she once walked, the same small town where her story began and ended. Her spirit touches this entire book.

In every chapter, you will find more than names and dates. You will find choices. Silences. Threads. And I hope you will find me.

Willie Jane Phillips (1908–1991) Born and laid to rest in Hillsboro, Coffee County, Tennessee A life rooted in the same soil, bookending the journey with hometown devotion.

She lived through world wars, the Great Depression, sweeping social change—and still, her story begins and ends in Hillsboro. That kind of local legacy has quiet power.

Holiday Hearth and Everyday Grace: Remembering Baba

What I remember most about Baba—Willie Jane Phillips—was going to her house for the holidays. We lived out in the country and rarely came into town, but when the holidays came, everyone gathered at her home in Hillsboro. Uncle Donald would drive down from Michigan City, Indiana, and all five of her children would be there with their families. Dad and Mom had five children, Virginia and Bill had four, Uncle Donald had two, Aunt

Shirley had two. Drenda was there too, daughter of James Dewey Anderson, who died serving in WWII. She was quite a bit older than us and had a child of her own. So, you can imagine, as we all grew older and began marrying, Baba's house was full of a growing, spirited crowd of cousins, laughter, and tradition.

Since I never knew Abb, her husband, Baba, was the only person I had to learn the family from. She was the heart and matriarch of it all.

She also took in boarders—men who rented rooms in her home. She cooked for them, kept their rooms tidy, and even washed their clothes. It helped her manage her expenses and stay busy.

I stayed with her sometimes, especially when we were quarantined with colds and viruses. She had already had them, so she could care for us when no one else could. I would walk to her house after school to mow her yard or tend the garden. Later, Mom would pick me up on her way home from work. Even when I got older, I still stopped by to help her when she needed it.

Toward the end of her life, her sister Aunt Mary moved in, as did her brother's widow, Aunt Ethel. I would check them from time to time, just as I did with Baba. It was part love, part routine—but always wanted to come home.

Two Teams and a Kitchen Full of Stories

By the time Baba was older, our family was big enough that when we gathered for holidays, we had *two full football teams* of cousins. It was not just backyard play, it was tradition. We would be outside running plays while the women bustled inside, cooking and getting everything ready. When the food was done, they would encourage us all to come in.

The seating order followed the old customs. The older men ate first, seated together at one table. Us children had our own table and stayed there until we were "old enough" to be invited to sit with the men. After the men finished, they moved on to the living room, and the women—finally—got their turn to eat. They would take over the main table, dishing their plates and settling in.

And that is when the real stories started. A whole lot of gossiping went on, some loud laughs, some quiet murmurs—it was their time to exhale and connect. And even after the football games wound down and the dishes were cleaned, the house stayed full of warmth. That was how it was done back then... and it worked simply fine.

Long Goodbye

Even as time moved on, Baba's house remained our holiday home. The drives into town became routine, but the heart of the gathering stayed the same.

Later in life, after she fell and broke her hip, things changed. She was in a lot of pain and spent most of her time settling into her recliner. I remember one visit clearly—she was playing a cassette tape of a preacher she liked, and I could tell she was tending to her soul, quietly preparing. I did not say anything. I just stayed close. I knew in my heart she was getting right with God, and I did not want to think about her leaving—just wanted to be with her a little longer.

After the fall, she gradually faded. Time gets slippery when you grow up, and I cannot recall exactly how long it was after that visit, but eventually she went into the hospital... and after a while, she passed.

Even now, she is with me. In my heart. In my soul. In my spirit.

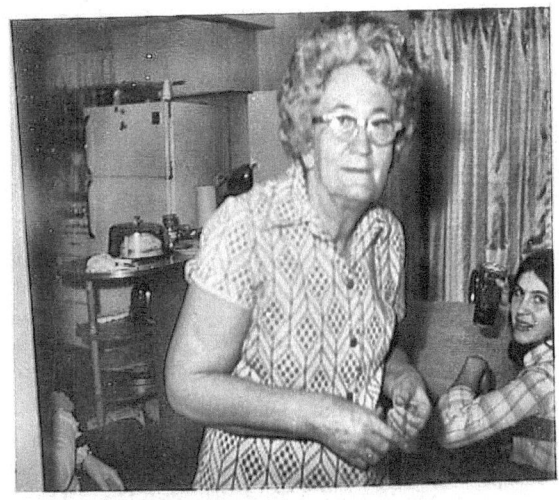

Willie Jane Phillips (Baba) 1908-1

*Brian Keith Anderson**

– *Final Stitch in the Phillips Quilt*

Brian Keith Anderson

Born: January 7, 1958, • McMinnville, Warren County, Tennessee **Status:** Living

Son of Robert Kenneth Anderson Sr. (1932–2015) and Helen Maxine Adams (1934–2004), Brian marks the continuation of three storied family lines—Anderson, Adams, and Phillips. Raised in Hillsboro, Tennessee, he grew amidst the echoes of ancestral faith and small-town grace.

A keeper of legacy and storyteller by calling, Brian dedicates his life to preserving history through narrative, image, and spiritual reflection. His work—woven with reverence and creativity—honors those who came before and inspires those still to come.

Robert Kenneth Anderson Sr.

Born: February 25, 1932, • Hillsboro, Coffee County, Tennessee **Died:** March 17, 2015, • Hillsboro, Coffee County, Tennessee

Son of Abb Anderson (1902–1951) and Willie Jane Phillips (1908–1991), Robert Kenneth Anderson Sr. was a lifelong resident of Hillsboro, Tennessee. A quiet steward of the family legacy, he carried forward the lineage with steadfast devotion to faith, family, and community. Married to Helen Maxine Adams in 1952, he became the father of five children: Robert Jr., Michael, Karen, Brian, and Kimberly. His life was rooted in the red clay of Coffee County and woven with love and quiet strength.

Willie Jane Phillips

Born: March 30, 1908, • Hillsboro, Coffee County, Tennessee **Died:** October 13, 1991, • Hillsboro, Coffee County, Tennessee

Daughter of Robert Calvin Phillips (1881–1942) and Gracie Ann Poff (1883–1948), Willie Jane was a lifelong resident of Hillsboro, Tennessee. Her life spanned eras of hardship and hope, and she bore witness to the evolving story of Coffee County from horseback days to humming highways. In 1925, she married Abb Anderson (1902–1951), and together they built a family rooted deeply in faith, work, and quiet endurance.

She was the mother of James Dewey, Lora Virginia, Robert Kenneth Sr., Donald Eugene, and Shirley Faye. Her strength lived in the rhythms of daily life: cooking from memory, tending with patience, and praying with unwavering trust. Her legacy endures in every story told at Sunday dinner, every photo framed on a descendant's wall, and the stillness of her resting place behind Hillsboro First United Methodist Church.

Robert Calvin Phillips

Born: August 22, 1881, • Hillsboro, Coffee County, Tennessee **Died:** March 8, 1942, • Hillsboro, Coffee County, Tennessee

Son of William Abraham Phillips (1856–1926) and Eliza Jane Pace (1860–1932), Robert Calvin Phillips was born and buried in the red-earth fields of Hillsboro. His life mirrored the turn-of-the-century Tennessee landscape: one of steady labor, faith-rooted simplicity, and familial devotion.

Married to Gracie Ann Poff on February 27, 1900, Robert fathered a dozen children, including Willie Jane—whose quiet strength shaped generations to come. Through farm seasons and family prayer, Robert lived with a blend of resilience and reverence, surviving loss and tending legacy.

His name remains etched in local soil and sacred memory—a patriarch whose lineage flows directly into your own pen strokes.

William Abraham Phillips

Born: September 1, 1856, • Hillsboro, Coffee County, Tennessee **Died:** March 16, 1926, • Hillsboro, Coffee County, Tennessee

Son of George Washington Phillips (1833–1915) and Martha E. Winton (1838–1900), William Abraham Phillips lived through a century's turning, bridging antebellum Tennessee and its rural resurgence. Married to Eliza Jane Pace in 1876, William's fathered a legacy of seven children: Robert Calvin, Bessie A., L.D., Fordy Webster, Cecil Movin, Mary Ola, and one still being named in memory.

A man of enduring soil and strong hands, William's life unfolded on the same Hillsboro land that became sacred with each generation laid to rest. His name threads through county census, family testimony, and now this written chronicle—a strong root beneath the branch that leads to you.

George Washington Phillips

Born: December 21, 1833, • Tennessee **Died:** August 1, 1915, • Hillsboro, Coffee County, Tennessee

Son of James Farris Phillips (1804–1889) and Rutha Casey Lusk (1808–1897), George Washington Phillips lived through the Civil War, Reconstruction, and the dawn of the 20th century. His life stretched across tumultuous times, yet his roots held firm in the clay and kinship of Coffee County.

He married Martha E. Winton (1838–1900) in 1855, and together they raised at least five children, including William Abraham Phillips—the line that leads to you. George fathered children with names like Ruthie, Robert Henry, and James F., each weaving another thread into this long Tennessee tapestry.

A man whose memory is often tied to handwritten census logs, faded gravestones, and Ancestry's tree branches, George represents endurance. His name lives now not only in records, but in this story—written fresh by his descendant, two centuries later.

⬜ *James Farris Phillips*

Born: March 28, 1804, • Amherst County, Virginia **Died:** December 24, 1889, • Hillsboro, Coffee County, Tennessee

Son of Johnson Phillips (1772–1847) and Nancy Grigsby Grady (1772–1839), James Farris Phillips was born in the green hills of Virginia and brought his young family westward to Tennessee, where generations now rest in Hillsboro soil.

He married Rutha Casey Lusk (1808–1897) in 1825, and together they raised a large, resilient family amid the shifting landscapes of antebellum America and Reconstruction. Their children, Elizabeth Jane, William Johnson, Sarah Grady, George Washington, Henry Alexander, Frances Marion, Robert Lacky, John Gilbert, James K. Polk, Joseph Dallas, Polly Caroline, and little Martha Amanda—formed the wide-reaching branches of a family tree that now blooms through your pen.

James lived to see eight decades of change, surviving loss and war while anchoring his family with quiet constancy. His memory lives in aged census records, weathered gravestones, and the faith carried forward by his descendants.

⬜ *Johnson Phillips*

Born: August 14, 1772, • Amherst County, Virginia **Died:** December 26, 1847, • Hillsboro, Coffee County, Tennessee

Son of John Phillips (1742–1795) and Avarilla Dickerson (1744–1795), Johnson Phillips was born in the early days of the American Republic. His life followed the rhythms of frontier movement—from the forested slopes of Virginia to the fertile fields of Coffee County, Tennessee.

He married Nancy Grigsby Grady (1772–1839) in 1792, and together they raised a large family that anchored faith, labor, and generational memory. Among their children was

14

James Farris Phillips, who extended their lineage into Hillsboro's red clay and became father to George Washington Phillips. Johnson's legacy now blooms through centuries of descendants, including you, Brian—a living branch still shaped by his migration, values, and quiet strength.

He is remembered through faded census records, old Virginia marriage registers, and the stone laid behind Wesley Chapel and Hillsboro First—where your sacred history continues to speak.

🍂 John Phillips

Born: May 28, 1742, • Orange County, Virginia **Died:** 1795 • Amherst County, Virginia

Son of Joseph Phillips (1710–1774) and Mary Bennett (1710–1775), John Phillips was born in the colonial wilds of Virginia, where tobacco fields stretched wide and revolution brewed quietly. His life marked a turning point in the Phillips story—nestled in the rolling hills of Orange County before planting roots in Amherst.

John married Avarilla Dickerson (1744–1795), with whom he raised a remarkable lineage: children bearing names like Hezekiah, Richard, Frances, Foster, and Johnson— the latter anchoring your direct line into Coffee County. From Virginia's shifting soil came a family that eventually crossed into Tennessee, carried by faith, grit, and generational calling.

Though his records live mostly in birth logs and aged family trees, his influence lingers in every branch that followed, including yours, written now in reverent ink.

Born: 1710 • England **Died:** 1774 • Surry County, North Carolina

Joseph Phillips was born in England at the dawn of the 18th century—a time when the Atlantic stood as both barrier and beckoning call. By the 1730s, he had arrived in colonial Virginia, settling first in Orange County before eventually establishing roots in Surry County, North Carolina.

He married Mary Bennett (1710–1775) on December 1, 1733, and together they raised a large family that spanned states and generations. Among their children were John Phillips (1742–1795), Bennett, Jane, Joseph Jr., William, David, Mary Ann, Elizabeth, Sarah, and Abraham—each a strand of the future web that extends to you.

Joseph's legacy is one of movement, settlement, and seed planting. His name threads through colonial registries, land records, and now this manuscript. In his courage to cross continents, your story found its roots.

🍂 William Phillips

Born: 1688 • North Farnham Parish, Richmond County, Virginia **Died:** 1739 • Virginia, USA

Son of William Phillips (1640–1725) and Susannah Williams (1669–1726), William Phillips was born beneath the steeples of colonial Virginia and spent his life amid its tobacco fields and parish halls. His family's presence in North Farnham marked them as early settlers in the region—a lineage already rich with migration, resilience, and quiet shaping of a country not yet born.

William married Ann Varichmond McWilliam Yates (1688–unknown), and together they raised several children, including Joseph Phillips (1710–1774), your seventh great-grandfather. Others in their branch include Leonard (1713), and Elizabeth (1717), whose births trace through parish registries like footprints in faded ink.

Though no formal monument may stand for him, William's legacy endures in the rippling generations of Phillips descendants—and in your manuscript, where his name now returns to light from the quiet of time.

⬚ *William Phillips*

Born: July 12, 1640, • Newport, Newport County, Rhode Island **Died:** December 1725 • Newport, Newport County, Rhode Island

Son of Richard Phillips and Frances Elizabeth Dryden, William Phillips was born in the heart of New England during its earliest colonial stirrings. His childhood would have unfolded amid Puritan towns and Atlantic winds, shaping a man ready for transatlantic ties and generational planting.

Though records place him chiefly in Newport, some entries trace key moments—such as marriage—to Braunton, Devon, England, suggesting familial or migratory ties spanning oceans. In 1685, he married Susannah Williams (1669–1726), and together they raised several children, including William Phillips (1688–1739), whose branch leads directly to you.

William's legacy lives not only in parish records but in the soil of Rhode Island, North Carolina, and Tennessee—migration braided through generations now woven in your story. It was a life of beginnings, echoes, and endurance.

Sir Richard Phillips (III Baronet)

Born: August 11, 1596, • Sutton Maddock, Shropshire, England **Died:** August 7, 1648, • Pembroke, Pembrokeshire, Wales

Son of John Richard Phillips and Margery Anna Raphes, *Sir Richard Phillips* was born into a lineage of distinction near the heartland of Shropshire, England. His title as Third

Baronet hints at both inheritance and responsibility—charged with estate management, social duty, and a role within the gentry of early Stuart Britain.

His final days unfolded in Pembrokeshire, Wales, where records point toward Picton Castle or nearby Slebech as burial locations. Whether through landed authority or quiet leadership, his name survives in aristocratic lists and echoes down to your own Tennessee branch—a thread unbroken through centuries.

Among his children were Erasmus, Ralph George, Katherine, Roger, Thomas, John, William (your eighth great-grandfather), and others who helped carry the Phillips name from British nobility to American soil.

Placed among ancestry and emblem, this crest speaks to the dignity carried forward— from baronets of Wales to hearts of Tennessee.

Coat of Arms of Sir Richard Phillips, III Baronet *Ducit Amor Patriae — "Love of Country Leads"* Framed in linen texture with sepia tones, this heraldic crest marks the legacy of Sir Richard Phillips, born in 1596 in Sutton Maddock, England. His title, lineage, and landholdings reflect a chapter of nobility that echoes across the centuries. The lion rampant symbolizes courage and guardianship; its stance on the escutcheon parallels the steadfast migration of the Phillips name across time and sea.

The plantation records, though fragmented and often incomplete, provide crucial clues to the family's life and the social structure within which they existed. These records detail not only the acreage of land owned, the types of crops cultivated (cotton, tobacco, or a combination thereof), and the livestock held, but also, and most distressingly, the enslaved population. Here, we confront the uncomfortable truth of our family history. The names of individuals held in the bondage are often listed, though frequently with minimal personal details. We are left with a sense of their existence, of their labor being integral to the economic success of the Phillips family, but with a profound lack of understanding of their individual lives, their hopes, their dreams, and their suffering.

A Promise Kept: The Story of Two Lines

Years ago, deep in my study of Johnson Phillips' line, a fellow researcher contacted me. He had traced the lineage of William Phillips, who had settled in Shelbyville, Bedford County, Tennessee—and noticed we shared kin. He told me a story passed down to him: five Phillips brothers came into the region, three went southeast, and two—William and John—laid down roots here.

He asked me if I would be willing to add William's line to my tree if he sent me the files. I said I would. A few days later, I received two plastic-bound folders: one marked "John Phillips Line," the other "William Phillips Line." Neatly printed, carefully placed.

Each morning before work, I added pages—first, Johnson's, then William's—fulfilling the promise I had made. I do not know how long it took. Only that I gave my word, and I kept it. John Phillips and Williams Jr. father was William Phillps Sr.

To me, it was not about building a tree. It was about remembering these people—and honoring my grandmother's lineage.

"Long before Hillsboro carried the Phillips name, Joseph Phillips stood in service to a budding nation. In return for his Revolutionary War commitment, he was granted the land that would become the cradle of a family's legacy—sixteen thousand acres, entrusted not merely to bloodline, but to principle. Through generations of marriage, devotion, and dispersal, the land dissolved—but the values it embodied endure in the lineage Willis Phillips bore forward."

Willie Jane's Father: A Life Rooted in Hillsboro

"She Carried His Legacy Forward" *The Life of Robert Calvin Phillips, as Remembered Through His Daughter Willie Jane*

Chapter Intro (Lead-In Paragraph):

Before the rows of lilies bloomed at Hillsboro First United Methodist Church, and long before the family quilts stitched generations together, there was a father—steady, unassuming, faithful. Willie Jane Phillips, born in Hillsboro on March 30, 1908, would carry his strength in her spine and his steadiness in her walk. She spoke of him not with grandeur but with gratitude: for the roots he gave her, for the soil that shaped him. Through her stories, the life of *Robert Calvin Phillips* unfolds—not just in birth and death, but in the gentle impact of a man whose legacy echoed quietly in the hearts of those he raised.

Robert Calvin Phillips/ nickname was (COW)

Born: August 22, 1881, • Hillsboro, Coffee County, Tennessee **Died:** March 8, 1942, • Hillsboro, Coffee County, Tennessee

Son of *William Abraham Phillips* (1856–1926) and *Eliza Jane Pace* (1860–1932), Robert Calvin was a lifelong resident of Hillsboro. He married *Gracie Ann Poff* on February 27, 1900, and together they built a large and enduring family, a living legacy of strength, tradition, and faith.

Robert's household blended siblings and half-siblings across Kentucky and Tennessee, shaping a family as wide as the seasons. He fathered children including *Dillard Frank*, *Ernest W.*, *Willie Jane*, *Lora Mae*, *Jessie D.*, *Mary P.*, and *Bobie Lee*, each name echoing through church pews and front porches long after his passing.

A man of quiet labor and community steadiness, Robert resided in Civil District 7, and later Huntsville, Alabama, before returning home. His burial in Hillsboro honors a full-circle life—born, lived, and laid to rest within the same sacred so

Beside Him, always: The Story of Gracie Ann Poff

Matriarch of the Phillips Line, Wife of Robert Calvin

Gracie Ann Poff

Born: May 10, 1883, • Hillsboro, Coffee County, Tennessee **Died:** October 10, 1948, • Hillsboro, Coffee County, Tennessee

The daughter of *James Marshall Poff* and *Harriet Julye McNutt*, Gracie Ann entered the world just before the loss of her mother in 1887. She would be raised among siblings and half-siblings stitched from early sorrow and resilience—*James Oliver*, *Lulu May*, *David Elmer*, *Blanche M.*, *Trudie Ethel*, and *Thomas B.*, each story threaded with triumph and tragedy.

On February 27, 1900, Gracie married *Robert Calvin Phillips*—and from that union sprang a legacy: seven children born and nurtured under Hillsboro's wide Tennessee sky, including *Willie Jane*, who carried her mother's memory with reverent pride.

Gracie's life was shaped by grief and grace, her years bookended by Hillsboro's familiar hills. Her strength lay not in proclamations, but in the quiet rhythm of raising children, mourning losses, and anchoring a family with unwavering love.

She is buried in Hillsboro, close to those she cherished, remembered not only for the life she lived, but for the lives she helped shape—her legacy preserved in pages and prayer.

Children:

Dillard Frank Phillips

Born: July 28, 1897, • Hillsboro, Coffee County, Tennessee **Died:** July 23, 1979, • Scott County, Tennessee

The eldest child of *Robert Calvin Phillips* and *Gracie Ann Poff*, Dillard Frank, was born in Hillsboro at close to the 19th century, a son of red soil and long shadows. His early years were spent among the tobacco fields and winding roads of Coffee County, before adulthood called him farther north—eventually to Scott County, Tennessee, where he made his life.

On March 29, 1920, in Marion County, Indiana, Dillard married *Elsie Martha Chambers* (1904–1986), and together they began a new branch of the Phillips tree. Their children included *James Paul*, lost tragically young in 1925; *Kenneth Lee*, born in Elgin, Tennessee in 1926; *Betty J.*, born circa 1931; and *Shirley Ann*, born circa 1937.

Dillard served his country with honor, registering for military service in 1918 at age 21. He witnessed deep family change—his siblings growing and departing, his parents passing, and the world reshaping itself repeatedly. Through all seasons, he remained tethered to the Phillips legacy, rooted even as he wandered. *Spouse: Elsie Martha Chambers*

Born: March 30, 1904, • Scott County, Tennessee **Died:** July 23, 1986, • Scott County, Tennessee

Married: March 29, 1920, Indianapolis, Marion County, Indiana

A woman of quiet strength and enduring devotion, Elsie and Dillard built their life amid the hills of Scott County, raising children who carried their legacy forward. She bore sorrow and joy with grace—mourning their firstborn, James Paul, and nurturing their lineage with steadfast love.

Ernest W. Phillips

Born: November 6, 1904, • Tennessee **Died:** July 5, 1968, • Hillsboro, Coffee County, Tennessee

The second son of *Robert Calvin Phillips* and *Gracie Ann Poff*, Ernest was born as the century turned—a child of Hillsboro soil and Phillips quietude. His upbringing threaded through the rhythms of Civil District 7, surrounded by siblings whose names echoed in church registers and local memory.

On March 7, 1925, Ernest married *Ethel Bradie Basham* (1908–2000), sealing a union that would weather eras of transformation. They settled for a time in Huntsville, Alabama, before returning to Coffee County, where the heart pulled and the family story remained anchored. By 1940, Ernest was listed as head of household, married, and a steady presence in the local census—his character etched not in headlines but in hearthstone routines.

He registered for the WWII draft as a middle-aged man, demonstrating a quiet readiness to serve even in life's later chapters. He outlived both parents, bore the losses of siblings gone too soon, and held memory's thread with dignified strength.

Ernest passed in Hillsboro and was laid to rest in the same familiar soil where he had been raised—a loop gently closed; a legacy tucked between the lines of rural Tennessee life.

Spouse: Ethel Bradie Basham

Born: April 25, 1908, • Hillsboro, Coffee County, Tennessee **Died:** February 3, 2000, • Hillsboro, Coffee County, Tennessee

Married: March 7, 1925, Coffee County, Tennessee

Ethel Bradie, raised among the red clay and quiet fields of Hillsboro, brought grace and resilience to the Phillips household. Married at seventeen, she and Ernest carved out a life marked by service, kinship, and rooted faith. Ethel outlived her husband over three decades, remaining in the town where their union first bloomed, a quiet matriarch whose presence lingered long after her passing.

Willie Jane Phillips

Born: March 30, 1908, • Hillsboro, Coffee County, Tennessee **Died:** October 13, 1991, • Hillsboro, Coffee County, Tennessee

The third-born child of *Robert Calvin Phillips* and *Gracie Ann Poff*, Willie Jane grew up within the rhythm of Civil District 7—among siblings who shared chores, hymns, and stories by firelight. Her roots ran deep in the Hillsboro soil, and her life reflected the steady grace she inherited from her parents.

On February 6, 1925, she married *Abb Anderson* (1902–1951) in Coffee County. Together, they built a family that spanned joy and sorrow—welcoming six children into the world: *James Dewey, Lora Virginia, Robert Kenneth, Donald Eugene,* and *Shirley Faye*. Each bore the imprint of her steady hand and the quiet strength of their Phillips heritage.

She outlived both husband and children—carrying their stories with reverence. Her home in Hillsboro remained the spiritual anchor for generations, her memory of a whispered grace passed from grandchildren to great-grandchildren.

Known for her gentle wisdom and unwavering faith, Willie Jane was laid to rest in Hillsboro near those who came before. Her legacy endures through the pages you are writing, Brian—and through the hearts she quietly shaped.

Spouse: Abb Anderson

Born: February 26, 1902, • Hillsboro, Coffee County, Tennessee **Died:** November 8, 1951, • Hillsboro, Coffee County, Tennessee

Married: February 6, 1925, Coffee County, Tennessee

Abb Anderson was a man of steady hands and soft-spoken integrity, married to Willie Jane Phillips in a union that anchored their lives in the red soil and tall pines of Hillsboro. Father of six, he bore grief with grace when their son James Dewey died in wartime service, and he cultivated a legacy marked by faith, toil, and devotion to kin. Though his life was cut short at forty-nine, the roots he lay in Hillsboro have held strong across generations.

● Lora Mae Phillips

Born: September 3, 1910, • Hillsboro, Coffee County, Tennessee **Died:** November 24, 1995, • Owens Crossroads, Madison County, Alabama

The fourth child of *Robert Calvin Phillips* and *Gracie Ann Poff*, Lora Mae was born into a home stitched with quiet faith and deep family ties. Her early years unfolded in Civil District 7, under the Tennessee sun, with siblings whose laughter and losses shaped her spirit.

On December 2, 1928, at age 18, she married *William F. Pylant* (1903–1985) in Madison County, Alabama. Together they raised a family of five, each child an echo of Lora Mae's gentle resilience: *Franklin* (b. circa 1931), *Wilma* (b. 1933), *Wanda F.* (1939–2009), and *Janice* (1945–2014). The family lived in Owens Crossroads for six decades, weaving Alabama roots from Tennessee threads.

Though she endured the loss of several siblings—including *Jessie D.*, *Bobie Lee*, and later *Ernest W.* and *Dillard Frank*—Lora Mae's grace never waned. She was the keeper of quiet strength, remembered for her nurturing warmth, her steady presence, and a voice that soothed across generations.

She passed away at age 85 and was laid to rest in Madison County, reunited with William, and surrounded by the gentle hills that had become home. Her legacy lives on— in the stories you preserve, Brian, and in every hand that touches your pages with love.

Spouse: William Franklin Pylant

Born: April 29, 1903, • Hurricane, Madison County, Alabama **Died:** June 18, 1985, • Madison, Madison County, Alabama

Married: December 2, 1928, Madison County, Alabama

Raised in Hurricane and rooted in the rhythms of Madison County, William was a steady presence beside Lora Mae Phillips. Together they nurtured a family of five—Franklin, Wilma, Wanda, Janice, and one unnamed child—guiding their household through decades of rural change and family growth. William's work was quiet but enduring, mirrored in the soil he tilled and the children he raised. His burial in Huntsville seals his story near the land he called home.

Jessie D. Phillips

Born: November 4, 1914, • Hillsboro, Coffee County, Tennessee **Died:** July 8, 1930, • Hillsboro, Coffee County, Tennessee

Sixth child of *Robert Calvin Phillips* and *Gracie Ann Poff*, Jessie entered the world beneath the same Hillsboro skies that would cradle his entire life. His childhood unfolded alongside siblings whose footsteps marked the same porches and pathways of Civil District 7—*Willie Jane*, *Lora Mae*, *Mary P.*, and others forming a circle of stories around him.

Jessie died tragically at age 15, a loss that left silence in the spaces where laughter once lingered. Family records place him in Huntsville, Alabama shortly before his death, for treatment or care, but he returned to Hillsboro where his journey ended. His passing was one of the deepest valleys Gracie and Robert would ever walk.

Buried in Hillsboro, close to kin and memory, Jessie remains a gentle echo in the family story reminder that some legacies bloom early, rooted not in years but in love that never forgets.

Mary P. Phillips

Born: August 21, 1919, • Hillsboro, Coffee County, Tennessee **Died:** January 9, 1981, • Hillsboro, Coffee County, Tennessee

Seventh-born child of *Robert Calvin Phillips* and *Gracie Ann Poff*, Mary arrived at the close of the First World War, into a home seasoned by love and loss. As a child in Civil District 7, she watched life unfold across Hillsboro's porches and plowed fields— growing up within the same rhythm that marked the Phillips-Poff legacy.

On November 12, 1938, she married *Sanford Kennedy* (1914–1970) in Coffee County, and together they carved out a life rooted in community and quiet devotion. Their daughter, *Linda Sue Kennedy* (1949–2016), born in Texas, brought a new chapter— blending the Tennessee heritage with paths farther west.

Spouse: Sanford Kennedy

Born: April 28, 1914, • Tennessee, USA **Died:** April 29, 1970, • Hillsboro, Coffee County, Tennessee

Married: November 12, 1938, • Coffee County, Tennessee **Spouse:** *Mary P. Phillips* (1919–1981)

Sanford grew up in the hills of Coffee County, one of ten children born to George Washington Kennedy and Nora Bell Sain. Married to Mary Phillips in the autumn of 1938, he settled in Hillsboro, where they raised a daughter, Linda Sue, born in Texas but rooted in the Tennessee spirit. Sanford lived quietly but meaningfully, a man remembered for his steadiness and devotion. He was laid to rest in the Methodist cemetery near the land that shaped his life—one day after his 56th birthday.

Mary endured profound loss with the deaths of her siblings—*Jessie D.* and *Bobie Lee* in youth, and others through the passing decades. She outlived both parents, holding tightly to the threads of their memory. Widowed in 1970, she continued in Hillsboro until her own passing in 1981, closing the final page of her generation's story.

She is buried in Hillsboro, close to the roots from which she grew—remembered as a woman of conviction, quiet strength, and lasting presence.

Bobie Lee Phillips

Born: October 26, 1923, • Coffee County, Tennessee **Died:** January 26, 1924, • Hillsboro, Coffee County, Tennessee

The youngest child of *Robert Calvin Phillips* and *Gracie Ann Poff*, Bobie Lee came into the world as autumn was fading and winter approaching. Her life lasted just three months—but even the briefest bloom leaves fragrance behind. Born at the close of the Phillips-Poff family expansion, she was held, named, and loved.

She passed on January 26, 1924, in Hillsboro, the place where her story began and ended. Though she left before memories could be made, Bobie Lee's name lives in family records, gravestones, and tender heart space. Her burial in Hillsboro marks a place of quiet reverence, near those who carried her memory and spoke her name.

Her life may have been short, but its inclusion in this manuscript ensures she is never forgotten.

Final Blessing

"From the dust of Hillsboro to the heavens beyond, may these stories rise like morning light—folded into memory, stitched with grace, and carried forward by love. This is the legacy of Phillips."

This book, like the land and faith that held them, was never just ink on paper, it is a prayer for remembrance. A tribute to those who tilled soil and bore sorrow, who sang hymns beneath pine trees and whispered blessings into baby ears. May future generations walk gently in their footsteps and feel the echoes of their names in the wind.

"The legacy of Phillips lives on." —B.K. Anderson

☐ Index of Names & Places